There Is No Finished World

There Is No Finished World

Leane —
with Thanks for your
interest in my work

Stephen Corey
9 February 2007

Poems by

Stephen Corey

WHITE PINE PRESS · BUFFALO, NEW YORK

White Pine Press, P. O. Box 236, Buffalo, New York 14201

ACKNOWLEDGMENTS: Poems from this collection have appeared previously, sometimes in a different form, in the periodicals appreciatively noted here:

88: A Journal of Poetry: "Abjuring Political Poetry," "Strengthening the Myth"; *Ascent*: "Universe"; *Atlanta Review*: "The Ghost of the Poet," "Seattle Merry-Go-Round"; *Controlled Burn*: "Know"; *Convergence*: "Where the Painting Is"; *The Devil's Millhopper*: "Book Reviewer"; *Great Stream Review*: "What the Road Said"; *The Hollins Critic*: "'Walk-ins Welcome'"; *Hurukan*: "Employment"; *The Kenyon Review*: "Measures"; *Kestrel*: "A String Around Your Finger," "No Beauty"; *The Laurel Review*: "One Night in Lima"; *New CollAge*: "What the Eagle Said"; *The New Review*: "The Sounds of Those Faithful," "Style," "20th-Century Skepticism"; *Poetry*: "Editing Poems During a Hospital Death Watch," "Poems of This Size"; *River City*: "1998: One Hundred Years Together," "Who Would Not Seek the Perfect Gesture of Love?"; *Runes*: "Carpe Diem"; *Shenandoah*: "Called Forward"; *Snake Nation Review*: "Apology to My Daughters, 20 and 17"; *Solo*: "Death Tricks," "Knotter," "Notes from the Year of My Father's Dying"; *The Southeast Review* (formerly *Sundog*): "Black Hole," "The Boy Scout's Motto Explodes," "Forgetting Mortality," "Trailer on Trailer on Trailer"; *Southern Humanities Review*: "Anything," "Emily Dickinson Considers Basketball," "My Daughter Playing Beethoven on My Chest," "To My Daughters at My Death"; *Tar River Poetry*: "One Answer"; *Yellow Silk*: "Living Hands"; *Yemassee*: "The Drive to Work."

   Poems from the fourth section appeared in a chapbook, *Mortal Fathers and Daughters* (1999), published by Palanquin Press of Aiken, South Carolina.

   "The Painting Comes Home" appeared first in *Heart to Heart: New Poems Inspired by Twentieth-Century American Art*, edited by Jan Greenberg (New York: Harry N. Abrams, Inc., 2001).

The lines by Woody Allen in "Employment" are from "The Irish Genius" in *Without Fathers* (Random House, 1975); the lines by Allen Ginsberg in "My Daughters' Photograph as a Bookmark in *Howl*" are from *Collected Poems 1947–1980*. Copyright 1955 by Allen Ginsberg. Reprinted by permission of HarperCollins Publishers Inc. The lines by Ted Kooser in "The Ghost of the Poet" are from "The Skeleton in the Closet" from *Sure Signs: New and Selected Poems* (University of Pittsburgh Press, 1980).

Publication of this book was made possible, in part,
by grants from the
National Endowment for the Arts
and with public funds from the
New York State Council on the Arts, a State Agency,
and by subvention funds from the
Center for Humanities and Arts at the University of Georgia.

Cover painting: "There Is No Finished World." André Masson (1896-1987).
Copyright ©2003 Artists Rights Society (ARS) , New York/ADAGP, Paris.

Printed and bound in the United States of America

First Edition

Library of Congress Control Number: 2003108947

Contents

In memory of
Stanley W. Lindberg (1939–2000),
great editor and friend.

There Is No Finished World

Knotter

n. 1. a person or thing that ties knots 2. a remover of knots

Henceforth I shall be the one
preparing strips of inflammable cloth,
wrapping pole torches that they might yield
an incandescent light, hours-long, to every needy moth.

Or perhaps I'll back up still farther,
will be the one breaking down
the gnarled pine-pitch torches, raveling
flammable wood strands to soak
in viscous resin for slow, candescent burning.

And then there's that old magician
I might be, with his elementary trick:
those complicated loopings-through of rope
followed by that double-handed, outward snap
you expect will bulk the knot up tight—
yet suddenly off it flows, water over rock,
leaving a pure straight line of twisted threads
old Karl Wallenda's ghost could dance across,
a horizon soft spring sun might lift above.

Understand

It's our job—while flipping burgers or turning
potters' wheels or tuning Ferraris—and
it's what we must do well or not at all:
no "sort of thinking of my death today" will do,
nor half-assed notions that your ass will soon be grass.
Be it day or swing or graveyard—what's in a name?—
every shift is one we're ready to take, one
we'll show up for, gripe about, and float through
till they set us loose or toss us out.
Over yonder's the unemployment line,
the one we'll all clock into down the road.
For now, we're working at the this-then-that-then-
this-again—a cycle sometimes the seconds
of an assembly line, sometimes the years
between inventive thoughts.
                              But all of it is,
as they say—this pumping gas, this
opening and closing of the heart, this
pounding of the beat with stick and gun—
a living.

Employment

I have a friend I have not seen
these dozen years or more, a man without his rightful work
because no job existed in America, not one,
for a Doctor of Philosophy
in Philosophy of Religion.
Just months before our final meeting
he'd read and thought and written
his way at last to that degree,
then found himself dead
center in the garish spotlight
suffered by Woody Allen's Liam Beamish,
who "could remove his false teeth and eat peanut brittle,
which he did every day for sixteen years
until someone told him there was no such profession."

Sporting the smooth elan of a stand-up comic
while his toddlers swarmed around him and the TV blared,
my friend would quick-talk tales of the world's bizarre believers:
the ascetic Pakistani hermit, living with arm outstretched
for years until it froze there, atrophied;
the famous grazing monks of Medieval France,
approaching Nature and God each morning
through a reverent, extended munching of the monastery grounds.

That last afternoon, we escaped upstairs to his bedroom
like eight-year-olds on the lam from a grown-ups' party.
He dug from his underwear drawer the prize
flea-market find his wife (they've since divorced)
would never let him hang, nor even speak of in her presence:
inside an overlarge, gilded wooden frame,
peering through twenty-odd ovals
trimmed from a once-white mat,
the tight-tuxedoed necks and dour looks

glued on the faces of the Class of '49,
Castleman School of Mortuary Science.

I still recall our lunatic remarks
addressed to those clean-shaven baby men
who'd already touched more dead than I would ever see,
who'd stood long-robed and marched in line
across some creaking stage to proclaim their skills with death.
All that we said soon left us
sprawled in hysterics on the double bed
as we spun out endless histories, past and future,
for the stalwart Castleman clan gone forth
in the year of Orwell's *1984*:
one became the Chief Embalmer
for Persians and poodles and cockatiels
entombed at L.A.'s Petland Heaven,
another left the business and street-hawked Oil of Olay
in the bench-filled parks of St. Petersburg, Fla.

He *did* find a job, of course,
and likely has it still,
counseling mothers and fathers
against beating their children.
His every word and look and hand through the air
might be fuel as easily as water—
another infant flipped against a wall.
It's never what we're trained for.
It's what we find, and make of it, and live with.

A String Around Your Finger

We forget so as not to be reminded
we used up such-and-such a time
doing this or that, spent twice as long
focused completely on that thing there
when we'd better have so-on-and-so-forth . . .

We cringe with delight at the weird
statistics surfacing here and there:
in a year we down seventeen pounds of sugar—
in a decade drink twenty-nine barrels of water—
the typical male, in a lifetime,
ejaculates two or three gallons.

What's done seems done, including all the tricks
baked in the language pie, if only we'd listen.
I'm well past forty now—can someone, please,
tell me the meaning of *hellbent-for-leather?*

The Great Mandala circles only once for each of us,
the wheel of fortune several times at best--
though some of us learn to spin
through untold revolutions
on our bodies' own thin axes
while we creak and grind along.

Some words break the rhythm of every line
you'd think to work them into: *orgasm*
is one of this ilk, leaving us lurching every time.
Do you recall your first, the way it split
your past and present like a ten-foot wall?
(*There*'s a man's question, she'll say.)

As I said, we'd never forget a thing
if we lived forever. All threats would be dead,
and all fears, so our burst-proof brains could fill
and fill until the cows came home and all the angels sang.

The Sounds of Those Faithful

Singing another world,
skewing their eyes for this . . .

clicking their dancing heels on pain,
on graves . . .
                    silently stuffing their ears
to close out the whispers of volition and chance . . . .

These are the sounds of those faithful
who attest that the future's air
weighs more than the dirt of now,
trust their very children's breaths
to the darkest distant waters,
and watch their own hands rising
first in front of their faces
and next toward the clouding sky—

who deny in each tensile moment
the lives of such occult braveries
as muscle and nerve and brain.

"Walk-Ins Welcome"

To go without appointment is the only hope.
Arrive when expected, by agreement,
and you're treated to be sent away—
your time comes, your time is done and gone.
Come randomly, uncalled for, and your prospects
multiply. You might be turned away—
"Yes, we know what the sign says,
but today is just impossible"—
or you might be embraced, grudgingly
or dearly. You might be ushered in
pronto, hair to be trimmed or infection staunched,
or you might sit waiting among the crowds
of the signed-up and others like yourself.
When finally called, you might be overcome
by gratefulness or exasperation, and
you might be greeted by same on the other side
of the perennial curtain or door.
When you leave—improved or not,
helped or not, repaired or not—
you need not feel the end is here
nor feel you must be gone for weeks
or months until your time comes round again.
You can click the door behind you,
turn to stare up at the still-lighted sign,
and walk back in.

Mr. Spudnut, giant geeky grin and slicked-back hair,
strode toward me, 3-D-ish, from the doughnut bag,
cradling in each arm a giant bag of doughnuts—
on each bag a junior Mr. Spudnut, geeky slick,
with two bags clutched in his spindly arms.
That's seven Mr. Spudnuts now, a lucky-number's worth . . .
except that I'm suddenly seeing those tiny other chaps,
riding their four little luggers' eight little hips
toward the edge of visibility—
and then, hugged by all these eight in turn,
I'm sensing and almost tasting
what have to be the tiniest doughnuts
ever in the world, lightly smushed inside
every one of those sixteen fingernail bags.

All those grinning men, all that paper and lard,
would appear in our kitchen occasionally,
borne by my early-up, sweet-toothed dad.
Then, several weeks ago, in the furious rush
defining the constant drone of any interstate,
a trailer on trailer on trailer
seemed to slide back toward me, growing
from dot to off-true square to what it was:
giant flatbed holding slightly smaller flatbed
holding propped-up, cabless body of a semi.
And yesterday, beside this same broad speedway,
a smashed and rusted auto hung by the cable
winched from a flat-tired, deeply canted wrecker—
and something in me wanted to pull right over
to join the little train, to lean my brittling spine
against the sun-hot hood of that pathetic truck, and wait.

What I Don't Understand

I had thought to begin with telephones,
how I heard this morning in Georgia
a woman's voice, clearly and simply, from southern France—
but I've decided now to start with lint
as it is gathered by the sackful in South Carolina,
bagged by many from the region's washing machines
and bought by one to be transformed into art:
lint sculpture sometimes, but usually lint collage
on paper, or lint mixed with paints on canvas or wood.

A grocery list is not a poem,
so I cannot hope to hold you here
endlessly rocked from page to page
in some high-falutin' litany
à la Sears & Roebuck or L. L. Bean;
we must have some development,
if only toward the obsolete
senses of *understand*: to prop up or support,
to know how to conduct oneself in proper form.

In high school chemistry we gathered words
to paste upon our brains as we watched
the shifts of color and state in tubes and beakers:
valence, bonding, molar and of course *molal,*
the *asymptote* toward *absolute zero.*
I carry these now in my head in the trusting way
I keep and peruse at night my senior annual,
block after block of faces and names
a quarter-century gone into versions
of whatever it is I've gone to myself.
Victoria Calamucci. Daniel and David
Christofferson. Jane Dale. Beverly Dawn
Fratelli. Beverley Jean Giroux.

What the Road Said

Always the hawks will be with me,
but their touch I will never know
except as an eye's-blink slash of shade.

No matter—trapped on the ground I fly
out and out ahead of you:
rod for the desert, snake for the mountain,
squares for your cities of loss.

I am escape, a mere dozen turns
to the far end of the country.
I am death in the dark
by leaping and crawling and racing,
am my own black armband uncoiling.

What the Eagle Said

Nail me to a chartreuse plywood door,
black ring welded to my belly.

Print me on a paper kite,
run me out, let me soar.

Star me in a foreign film,
glorious nymphs sucking my claws.

Ice me across your cake, tricolored.

Plot my weave and gleaming
into every seat and mirror.

Make me mushroom, and mushroom again.
I'll ride you all out, and over,
updraft and down.

One Answer

Let us not overrun ourselves with bullshit
that lauds all lives as equal, nor with nonsense
that sets nobility lurking in every act and word.
If a thing or action is not in your dreams
for the life you wish to lead, it is not good for you;
if it lives in no one's lofty plans
it is not good for anyone at all.
When I drove a main-but-rural highway
in the literally blistering August Georgia sun,
I saw near the pumps of a crossroads station
an aging man, in dingy coveralls, push-brooming sandy dirt
toward the roadside ditch from the gas-rank, greasy concrete.
I thought, "My God, what a place and job
to have six decades come to." And I was not
insensitive or elitist or judging without sufficient facts.
I was simply, for once in my life, correct.

Universe

The one turning is all we seek:
a warm noon breeze at winter's end,
the child's fever breaking in time,
the single pair of eyes our way
in the overcrowded room—
their depth-gaze proclaiming
we are, beyond all doubt,
the one. Turning is all we seek:
butter from milk, hawk in gyre,
leaf in whirlpool, steel from fire,
many strong backs against violence and war,
old prejudice into respect for
the one turning. Is all we seek
a shift from sameness, the grave's precursor
Poe saw daily in his canted mirror?
Or do we wish for change like God's, all
revolving and evolving within the great bubble
the one turning is? All we seek
drives us to question the sought—
what worth this canvas daubed with paint,
this debit to the ledger, this rush of blood
in bed or birth or slaughter?
How long can we move ourselves to believe
the one turning is all? We seek
the change that does not mean the end—
aloneness into love, dullness to arousal,
flat brown fields to gauze of sprouting green—
the change that primes and perks us
for the world, mutes the narrow notion
the one turning is all *we*. Seek
and ye shall seek—*there's* a turn
that turns a phrase our way.
We have pancakes and pirouettes,

Satan's anus-gate to heaven,
hot to cold, elation to despair,
rock to lava to rock.
We have the child's first smile, first step, first word.
And everywhere we look we look, and
the one turning is all we seek.

Poems of This Size

Poems of This Size

In poems of this size, so little
might happen, one wonders if such brevity
can matter—as when I strolled, thirty years ago,
with my wife (a year before she *was* my wife)
in her first neighborhood, and we heard
that familiar, horrible squealing of tires down the block.
And because she was a young nurse, no doctor
in sight, when we reached the small boy
lying on the red-brick street with many people
gathered around, *she* had to step forward and kneel,
had to be the one cradling him and wondering,
most closely, at how quick and full an end can be.

Carpe Diem

I want the mind of Emerson
at the moment of his first masturbation,
Dickinson faced with the bloody cloth,
all the genius children of the world
when their bodies grabbed their throats
and squeezed into silence those beautifully windy brains.

The Boy Scout's Motto Explodes

No matter all the myths of departure
and return, all of nature's taut cycles,
all holidays and anniversaries
through my full half-century of breathing
in and out, quick and slow, deep and shallow,
still there's no name for my daughter's breast milk
bottled in my dry hand, this nourishment expressed
for my grandson's delight and survival
in my arms while she is absent—she to be known
soon to him as mother, she I once knew
as a sleeping white cocoon of blanket
beside *her* mother—whose then-hard breast I tongued
to give relief and, it seems today, to prompt a world.

Black Hole

Because, as Kathryn Kuhlman said,
"All things are possible with God,"
it's possible the earth is God's
black hole, the feed-in point for all
that is, dense ball of being
in the great dark flat of nothing's
amniotic vacuum sack. French fries
are here, and French Impressionists,
and string, and rotting liver, too.
Out there—blank, and blank, and blank.
God sucked it in. We need not reach
for what's beyond. It's not.

20th-Century Skepticism, or,
Another Idea Succumbs to Art and Truth

"After all one isn't a potato."
—Edward Lear

A brazen new theory this old queery-Leary
put forth in a century past,
to posit that you, sir, were not born a tuber
whose works could be baked, fried, or mashed.

Such quick metaphysic that starch-collared critic
might sneak past those duller than we,
but *we* know as poets our job is to show it's
not easy to slice *a* from *b.*

Style

The hair itself is one
dictator: the single strand's thickness,
the density of strands,
their straightness or kink or wave.

And color:
can gray live the life of black,
brown make auburn's moves?

Then, the skull and flesh
the hair must lie upon, shift across.

Even the world itself:
what winds, what light and moisture
to affect the look?

And who might notice, and who might touch?
These are a part of the fashioning,
the linking of *must* and *could* and *will*.

Always one answer
sought. Never
one answer given.

Know

This is the one in which I know nothing:

The count of the lines of my visible blood—
thin and thick, ankle and hand.

Exquisite arousal, again and again,
from the close-filmed sex of strangers.

My too-young daughter at my father's coffin,
asking where his belly had gone.

Footprints I cannot leave behind
in a state where snow is always rain.

Really, Medusa's the easy way out,
those snakes for hair a weak side glance
at what needed seeing. Hair is merely decorative,
merely dead. Let's have snakes from the throat
roiling out over the lips, or snakes from the anus,
or maybe one snake from each eye.

My grandpa, one hundred and one, shuffles
the small green corridor, catheter
trailing—they're wed now forever, these two.
Tendons still course his body, but with power
no longer their name, nor tautness their gift.

Dear god, we should say, make us rock.
Cast not upon us again thine eye
that lets us go soft, lets us rot.

Editing Poems During a Hospital Deathwatch

Dear Poet:
I'm sorry, but I couldn't use your art
today to soothe or distract me from this death—
not quite accomplished yet, but pressing out
as twitchings of her cold and curling feet,
as ulcerous brown blood seeping with her breath.
I expect, had you known, you might have sent
something more attuned to the current path
my mother-in-law is facing. I'm sure
you're thinking this private critique unfair,
and you'd be right to be upset, except
that you'd be wrong. This place, right here, is where
we *always* meet: Beatrice with her chart
devoid of final blessings, you and I
searching for the words that nail sensation to the sky.

Measures

Measures

I knew a woman
who wouldn't trust a man
who wouldn't eat zucchini plain—
something about simplicity,
readiness to live far down
the line from blood and thundering.

The oddest measures
have ways of ensuring
truth is wrung from complexity,
she said. No lies with zucchini,
she said. And no preening. No murders.

Her angora, purring,
would sprawl its silken fur
across us both, limply—
chest on my thigh, belly on hers.
In all the muscles, such serenity.

Bobcat, lynx, cougar, lion—
all, of course, were *kitten*
once, she said. That's given.
And a man's eye when he sees them,
or hears that word—she'd know him then.

Living Hands

—*See, here it is*—
I hold it towards you

They stood, sides touching, and stared at the hand of Keats
open to them there behind the glass, its movements a map
inscribing what otherwise none (save John) could sense:
the pulsings and shiftings of the only brain ever
to form that strange and massive shell, *Endymion*,
now thus beached before these two by countless quirks of histories.

We, the knowing watchers of these lookers, must wonder
how their own felt thoughts, on beauty or art or death, might
      differ
had not the couple just an hour (and two) ago been making love
with a wired intensity long unfamiliar to both—
so that while they gaped at that ink two centuries old,
that paper more durable not only than flesh but than bone,
her body leaked their moisture into her clothing
and the dampness of his still tingled
while thick crowds milled and paused throughout
the Romantic exhibit, with its cluster of clear enclosures
showing off the passionate hands of so many
to the eyes of so many more.

And that could be one ending to the story, that "more,"
and you out there might turn away to think nine hundred things,
perhaps among them these:

      Will there never be an end to poems invoking Keats?

      I was, I must admit, slightly aroused by those later lines.

Is that "they" a transparent screen for "we,"
or did the poet observe and conjure—or conjure whole?

What you could not think to ask was whether, as I wrote,
a woman—unexpected—came to me with a warm and scented
      cloth
which I might press against my hands and face and neck,
thus bringing me back from body-in-mind to body
while the darkened ocean rolled backwards beneath me, six
      miles down
below our jumbo jet aimed toward a country I'd never seen—
and where I'd set forth to alter my life

in ways this poem has no chance of encompassing.
But I'm telling you she did, and though I've never seen her
      again,
she helped me to know what I must have sensed already: the tale
could not be finished, since *no* satisfactory story
encompassing stone lions could possibly end without those lions
ever coming to the page.

              Of course: the statues outside the exhibit hall,
ones the lovers did not think twice about, or so the man
      would have said
if asked before the woman's letter came some weeks beyond
      that day—
the letter that said she knew, or felt she knew, he hadn't known
the lengths to which her body would have gone that afternoon,
      that moment
when she pressed her hip to his and read

> *. . . we will shade*
> *Ourselves whole summers by a river glade;*
> *And I will tell thee stories of the sky,*
> *And breathe thee whispers of its minstrelsy.*

She would, she said, have fucked him at that moment on those
        lions,
either or both, and no need to clear the crowds away.

And so, having sworn he'd always trust her,
he entered a life that had at least one reality
he felt as more fantastic than his fantasies;
at oddest moments he would enter that truth, to picture

her seated, naked, on the narrow ledge by a lion's crouched legs.
He lifted the crooks of his elbows into those of her knees
to raise her, while she reached out to clutch him,
to pull him toward and into her, and all
the while the crowds might have *their* wills, too—
for those others did not, could not, matter.

I have no proof, as always, but some something tells me
it's more than accident that broke this poem in half,
that left me stranded for weeks on that harsh word, *fuck*,
and wouldn't free us all into what has followed
until I took to the air again, bound that time
for a nearer and far less curious city—though one,
I'd learned, where I'd likely encounter a woman
lost to my life for more than a decade, a woman
who had proven for me then, if anyone could, this anecdote
I'd later heard of the lion letter might be true.

No, I've got no stories to tell of that woman.
Rather, now might be the time to take more questions,
or to bring back that long-stranded, still-pulsing
hand of Keats, as if *it* held the answers
we want—or pretend—to seek. But in fact there's nothing left,
not even the time-warp tale I once set forth into plotting:

In that one, a poet without belief beheld an angel
who offered him the chance to sacrifice his life
to bring Keats back to breathe and write
for three-score-years-and-ten, or more.
That agnostic poet paused, trying to imagine what Keats
          could write
in the shadow of the year 2000, or whether he'd write at all.
Staring at the angel, unable to answer its question
on his own, he knew for the first time in his life
that whatever he did would be equally—absolutely—right
and wrong. Finally, in this story that never quite existed,
he closed and clenched his fists, and closed his eyes to the angel.

Many times I've made love desperate
over the moment or fate of the love,
but I'd never made love desperate
over life, over the world beyond the window,
until choked for a week on the gray-brown sludge
called air in that rank, bastard child of Pizarro.

The streets were plugged with the grinding and dying
cars of other nations: mufflers, even headlights, were dreams
in the ears and nerves of visitors;
a catalytic converter drew the biggest laugh
for the stand-up comic at the luxury hotel.
Vehicles of every axle and weight were stacked
toward the acidic sky, hollow ingots
coughing out their rusty and floating revenge.

Tiny mountain Indians, sucked down into the city
by lighted noise that seemed like food and work,
sat against the walls five storeys below us.
Across the babies sleeping in their laps, they held
cupped palms and, in a language not our own,
whispered and pled what we could not hear at all
from bed, yet heard and understood completely.

And so we came to know something of sex
in sub-Saharan tents while your children starve beside you,
of rolling and moaning with a guilt so huge
you let it go absolutely, as if sweating
and coming were some god's truest offering of peace.

1998: One Hundred Years Together

for Mary

We are a century now—and though
the merest far-cry shadow to my grandpa,
who'll next year be his own 100,
our whole of equal parts is still
a source for me of, frankly, wonder.
Alone, I would be merely fifty,
yourself unlinked the same—
just fifty-fifty, just two wandering *I*'s
left to chance, to this-or-that, to
eggless ham and yinless yang.

Our quartet of daughters—the numbers cannot lie—
add up this very year to a full life lived:
twenty-eight, twenty-five, eleven, and six
make the infamous three-score and ten.
There is not quite a symbol here,
not quite a meaning for the ages—
but, at the least, another moment's lesson:
anniversaries are such as we declare.
Our infants' ages we declaim in days at first,
then weeks and months and then half-years
before we settle for the sun's demanding
circuit, trimming our allotment back and back.

My dear, recall there was only a single day
in our 18,000-plus apiece
when we'd made love just once together:
before that one day, never;
the next, the count continued.

In American deserts the century plant
blooms once and dies—but the flower comes

49

after ten to thirty years. Was it named
by someone stupid, impatient, or wise?
Who could have been there at the breaking through
from the crust of rocky sand, then settled in
for the seemingly endless growth
and maturing of the nameless *agave*?
Who could have held that chain of days
together with no knowing where
or to what it all might lead?

Yet here we are, one hundred together
by a count we'll let none put asunder.
Agave means illustrious,
versary turning, *anni* a year at a time.
We must learn when to let things wander,
learn when to make them rhyme.

Who Would Not Seek the Perfect Gesture of Love?

Never was there anything enough to say . . .
yet once there I was,
watching the back of your head
and the left side of your jaw line
from my seat behind you on the crowded bus
as you gazed out the window,
there in that time when I was
brought into your presence, by our work
and by chance, for a week after years
apart, years of what they call nothing,
but of course was unable to touch you
since I had no rights in the world
outside of our fractured hearts—
and as I watched, a stray blacksilver hair
waved and swayed apart from the rest,
a cracked limb dangling in wind
like the wand of a fairy or the scepter of a priest
offering its foreign blessing
to one who dares approach.

I reached over the seat back; you still stared
away. My hand passed above your right
shoulder and alongside your neck,
opposite the window. I caught the thread
(younger and smarter I'd have called it *angelic*)
in the pincer of two empty fingers
to lift it away—a tiny blemish,
a flaw that could float on air.

Mortal Fathers and Daughters

Anything

"Do you file your nails?"
"Why . . . yes."
"Some people will save anything."
    —one of Uncle Jim's countless jokes

How about this small square napkin,
in my lap five miles from the earth
as we hum toward Lima to adopt an infant girl
we've never seen, or even heard described?
Might there be enshrinement in the air
this moment, in the American Airlines double-*A* imprinted
between thick bars extending across the delicate paper?
Crumpled and abandoned, it's gone within days
to landfill or burning; properly covered and laid away,
thinner than eyelid or veil,
it's somewhere intact when I am gone to bone.

I, not one who weeps, would weep
one day, I'm sure—not for a napkin
perhaps, but certainly for strands of hair
taped down in a scrapbook beside it: hair of Catherine,
invisible child-to-be, or of the older others,
three more daughters and a single wife.
Or even hairs I might not recognize,
through fault of sight or memory,
and perhaps they'd be something else entirely—
say, garment threads of black and brown
coiling upon themselves and offering
no hints to where they came from, but only
what we'd know already: that everything
pressed and preserved on these pages
turns to emblem, has no hope of ever being
itself again.

I am past the danger point here,

launched into sentiment I see
no way to funnel out of easily.
Of course, there *is* that element I missed
in my napkin logo, those geometric wings
close above the double *A:* trapezoids
angled so the one behind is broken,
its tiny lower tip jutting at the left—an eagle's tail—
and the bottom of the front one is notched
to be the stretched-forth talons in descent.
Perhaps we might save these wings alone,
trim them free with moustache scissors
like a photo cut down for a locket,
then tape them dead-center of an album sheet—
there to be found some year and compared,
in their crossing, to the perfect fingers
an oblivious newborn waggles in her sleep,
or to the countless sets of woven veins
in the electric muscle of the heart—
that lives its lifetime buried,
that we only dream of bringing into light.

Death Tricks

Because we give the earth our dead, we believe
it can hold anything.
Burial equals gone: father or nuclear waste,
we watch it go down, then turn away
to stay alive. I watched my fingers putrefy
as they lay on my thigh one full-moon night
while I sat on my back porch steps;
my flesh gave off that smell I've never smelled,
the one police describe as the thing
you can never imagine beforehand.

Thousands lie drugged and dying
in the carpetless rooms of city streets,
others grow deeply and lastingly rich
shaping perfect replicas of gun-shot faces
to be filmed for our viewing pleasure.

My father's corpse at my back, I chatted
with friends and a few strangers—
this is called *condolence*, from the Latin
condolens, "to suffer with"—
until my daughter, twelve years old,
asked where his stomach had gone.
And of course she was right:
already they were changing the story,
taking him from us—already
he was younger, sleek for the flight.

My Daughter Playing Beethoven on My Chest

—*for Rebecca*

She was nine, on the absolute edge
between her dying childhood and
that confusing ecstasy to come
then go in another decade's rush.

We were simply chattering—I
seated and she standing before me, she
spinning those silly child's nonsense tales
still lingering, circular repeating
jabberings a part of me laughs and loves
to hear, though often I am quickly bored,
annoyed, wishing to escape the wishing
her fantasy of words and voices means—
when suddenly her hands came forward and up,
spread like claws or the reach of a smaller child
playing ghosts or monsters. But her fingers kept coming
and lit upon my chest, ever so briefly
still, then launched into a spidery dance
of side to side, of up and down—
Beethoven's "Ode to Joy" thrummed above my lungs
as if she were typing out a secret
well-known message.
                            No, I could not decipher
that music's motion, upside-down and silent.
She hummed as well, her fully childish voice
releasing that long-ago tale of maturity,
as if it were the simplest thing of all
to offer up the musings of a genius.

What she played I could not play,
my hands from earliest days fat hams
stuck to the platter of my thinking,

music's flags and circles a Russian I could not read.
But I'd had ear enough to follow
the lead of her growing fingers—
at seven, then eight, then nine—on the keys,
which led to hammers and wires and board,
which had lifted sound through our every room and wall.

It's one thing to be clever about death,
as in tossing off the notion that you wear it
every day around your wrist. It's something else
to wake and be wearing it there.

✻

What the blueprints fail to show is the slum
this beautiful home, unbuilt, will become.

✻

I am four or five, my father proposes
a weeks-long reading of mysterious tales
whose inhabitants' very names are wonder:
Mowgli, Shere-Khan. I am ready
for each night's fragment, live
in full belief that tomorrow's piece
will be perfectly trailed by the next . . .

✻

Stunning what little we'll hold of a life
and think we're somewhere near it.

✻

And what is the answer from shower-stall tiles,
the fine ivory lines of grouting
beaded with water and perfect as health?
Slowly, you wash your body for the dead
one who is out there waiting.

*

. . . it will tear
our eyes and lips to the very end.

*

Watch unstrapped and squeezed in hand, I'm the boy
in the back seat in contest with himself,
holding his breath in the hot wind's roaring
while his family hurtles on without knowing
I have ceased, for now, the act of life.

*

Now the earth fills with the known,
mystery dissolved by monogrammed gold:
the tie tack with its gothic letters, DBC,
clasped and clasped by the dark vacuum.

*

And then there is nothing but death
as we suddenly learn of the masks
the middle-aged had worn when we were children,
showing us ease and comfort we took for real.

*

We must have a code
for the time when silence comes.

Apology to My Daughters, 20 and 17

Forgive me—I am really trying, each day, to be older.
I know the summer barings of my hairless thighs have shamed you,
and my endless jokes in the presence of your friends.
I know your bodies are adult, know the heads
turned and cocked our way these days when we walk together.
But look—these veins in my forehead, strained and filling
as I will my scalp to drop more hair into oblivion;
and note—last week I did not touch your mother even once.

Yes, I've been given *my* father's place in line,
and yes, you've caught me peeking backwards,
nodding at eager others to move on past.
But my diastolic hasn't dropped again in months,
nor my weight—so hope *is* springing, and always
my good intentions toward collapse.
I know you need some space, a gap to fill.

Last week new wrinkles jabbered from the mirror,
pitching for laughs to swell their sideshow ranks;
I could not bring myself listen to their spiel.
Twenty years ago I refused a war, denied
surrendering my gravest choices to another.
Perhaps that was the same? Yes, the war went on
despite me—so, I know, *Take a lesson, will you, dad?*—

But wait—that war bit was a trick.
My lithe, impatient ones, greatest obstacles ever
to my steely disbelief in God, forgive me:
now, our war is everywhere—no lotteries for luck,
no alternate service remaining
for the conscientious of any stripe or age.
The battles are in breathing, eating, loving.

I've purchased, on time, my own quiet plot—
yet am lustful and romantic as always,
am running my daily miles in the deadly sun.
My Lynn, my Dawn—I fear we will all die young.

Called Forward

Dale B. Corey, 1925-1985
Emily Dickinson, 1830-1886

Other poets to my father's grave
most certainly have never come;
to Dickinson's Amherst kingdom,
iron-fenced, they've trudged in iambic waves.
And so I owe my poem to him—
yet pay it now to her, most fierce
in genius, cold and warm and sparse,
who speaks above his silent din.
She saw his face and bones, born then gone
century and century beyond her;
she spoke his love, his chill, his stupor—
she taught me *grief is tongueless*, gave me song.

My Daughters' Photograph as a Bookmark in Howl

All I have at hand for the long flight,
dug from my book-filled backpack it becomes
the marker for this chapter in my life of reading:
these four together—two women, two girls—
with twenty-one years between oldest and babe,
all primmed and posed and primed for the eldest's wedding.

> *angelheaded hipsters burning for the ancient heavenly*
> *connection . . .*

Their backdrop the deep false blue so favored
by gallant commercial photographers,
this is the endless array of our daughters:
twenty-four, twenty-one, seven, and three,
skins from cherubic Swedish pink to Asian
palest olive to Andean mestizo brown.

> *who wandered around and around at midnight in the*
> *railroad yard wondering where to go, and went,*
> *leaving no broken hearts . . .*

Surrounding this chemical miracle
rolled moments and hours not to be lost
on the older two until infirmity:
Heather the bride, with rights to this day
as its shining center, this one day
when all would turn and stand and nearly bow,
this day when the heavy wooden doors
and the stained-glass windows of perception are cleansed;
Miranda the honored maid, caught by the web of the past
and the mirror of the future at once,
forced to turn away in tears when the aisle filled

with her familiar sister's radiance.

> *who cut their wrists three times successively unsuccess-*
> *fully, gave up and were forced to open antique*
> *stores where they thought they were growing*
> *old and cried . . .*

This portrait that will surprise the younger two
in years to come, their flourishing brain cells
ripe at three and seven for permanent filing
(until infirmity) of words and inflections and sentences,
of spellings and plots and processes and arcane detail,
but not yet ready to hold the larger events
so laden, we'll tell them later, with something
we call significance, the parent of nostalgia.

> *Moloch! Solitude! Filth! Ugliness! Ashcans and unob-*
> *tainable dollars! Children screaming under the*
> *stairways! Boys sobbing in armies! Old men*
> *weeping in the parks!*

This famous *Howl* I hold is worlds
these women/girls will likely never know—
world of ecstatic suffering,
world of suffering made ecstatic art—
for they are not bound toward impoverished dissolution,
nor likely to follow their father
on his voyeur's journey through the text
toward many worlds *he* will likely never know.

> *who fell on their knees in hopeless cathedrals praying*
> *for each other's salvation and light and breasts,*
> *until the soul illuminated its hair for a second . . .*

Yet here they are, showing there is no limit
to what might align *in the total animal soup of time*:
lace and nervousness and innocence,
in the faces of these four I've known
since all they could do was lie in a single place,
is captured here on paper and pressed against paper
where the faculties of the skull no longer admit
the worms of the senses;
and Ginsberg's vision (which is not his) is proven and disproven
in this instant of beauty which is and is no more;
and my daughters, sealed in this *Howl* as in a crevasse,
are at once released as on a huge, rising balloon
whose sound at bursting will be so far away and small
we can only imagine how near and great it must be.

All italicized lines and phrases are from *Howl* by Allen Ginsberg.

No Beauty

This once, it must not turn beautiful.

No, I don't mean another bucket
dampened with crocodile tears,
musty and ripe for scattering
to the impoverished tens of thousands
rocking and keening in the dust,
to the millions starving
far from the smell of ink.

I mean, no beauty close to home,
where every zero counts and burns each day:

My oldest daughter, fear in her eyes
when a man she's never met
reaches out along the crowded bar
to grab her wrist and hold,
to drill his stares at her face
while he wishes them hands at her crotch . . .

My adopted youngest, fresh from the triumph
that walking becomes for parent and child alike,
dreaming with no conception of dreams
the life she might have stayed with
in the arms of her child-mother,
wandering meek and filthy
the desert streets of Lima, Peru . . .

My wife, at work with her cooling dead,
occasionally two or three per shift:
how the time must come for the silenced or wailing
families to step outside the room,
to slough themselves away

that she may plug and wrap and bag
what had had a memory, a certain tone of voice.

Here is where we feel and know,
there where we think and pretend.
Music and wit are not exempt from limit.
A terrible beauty is merely terrible.

Dirt

Dirt. There, and back there,
and over beyond. It holds,
lets grow, gullies, dries.
And here: my father's grave.

To My Daughters at My Death

Forgive me for grouping you again—
I have never done so lightly,
would speak to you singly now
if such would make more sense.
But I know you are gathered
in that clutch we made of you,
that clowder and murder and pride
we failed to see we were building
in the shine of all that we loved you, one by one.

Yet I am not here, and am not here
to say such glowing, tinted things.
You are reading me, I've guessed,
as a breathing quartet—four of anything
or a group engaged in music . . .
but there I go again, averting
even my dead eyes and trying
to divert your pooling thoughts
from this one sheet and all of me
you hold in hand. And hand. And hand. And hand.

The matter, I feel, is this:
what did I withhold as I tried to give,
what broke on the circles I presumed to close
with this second language I learned
when the first, my life, became a spell
too convoluted for my breaking?
Did I turn from you in the paltry name of art,
diminish you for the silly sham of wisdom?
My wise beauties—
    Heather of hardy flowering,
    Miranda of vision and wonder,

Rebecca of searching and strength,
Catherine of purity—
                 my wise beauties,
where have we left ourselves now that we're possessed
by the separate worlds we'd only feared or ignored,
now that I have no hand to touch your hands?

So much I missed of all you did and thought,
but now I miss it all: raise or lower your eyes
in trust or question or anger, and remember
I will not see. And wonder, can there be such sights
wherever I might be now? Do I still know
the shading and shift of light in the delicate iris?
Pray for me, who never taught you how to pray,
that such a chilling, shivering thing might be.

Stone As Stone

Some men will shoot an infant in the face.
There, that's a start—near pentameter, even.
Has the world been bettered yet, or your mood?

The only mirror of horror is itself.
Art's a game when it thinks it shows the world
in actuality; art's a savior
when it stalks the world as art: stone as stone,
paint as paint, words as the music of words.

Here's a joke we children laughed at once:
What's the difference between a truckload
of bowling balls and one of dead babies?
You can't unload the balls with a pitchfork.

It's okay to laugh—that shows you sense the awfulness.
Imagine the hearer who did not get the joke:
No poem could reach him. No horror. No world.

The Drive to Work

On the daybreak sidewalk far ahead
she was motion you catch like a smell—
there, but sourceless till you crane and search.
She spun a full three-sixty on her toes:
arm and trunk a perfect T, head
snapped through to hold the balance-line,
long dress following in a slowly circling wake.

In the second that grace required, I neared
by the fifty feet my silent engine pulled me on.
Still faceless, she curled her bare arms
inward to her chest, the backs of her fingers
touching there and gliding straight back out
to signal the start of the next pirouette.
Five she managed before I rolled on past,
her raised toes holding every time
a single spot on the gritty cement.
On the last two turns I finally saw her face,
its sixty-odd years a sharp revision
to my guess her flow and body had supplied.

How little we know, but here is one thing
true: that woman never knew I passed,
knew only something else entirely.

I get around, yet needed forty years and more
to find an aging woman twirling by the road
for whatever fullness or emptiness
in a space she had defined,
a space that ran from breastbone to horizon—
hers, though the air that fueled her were better left
          unbreathed,

though the leaves above her may be dying far too soon,
though the ground beneath her toes is cousin to gaping caverns
imploded in the desert, two thousand miles away.

Seattle Merry-Go-Round

—for Jennifer

Not what one would think, not the ready-made
comfort and stasis of endless whirling
seamlessly joined with dip and rise.
Not the cone-roofed, light-strung, callioped building
heard and sighted from a distance. Not shrieking
children nor befuddled infants, not lovers with hands
goofily linked and rippling through
the down-up-down of adjacent horses—
lovers with groins triggered for the night
by the press of wooden backs, by the rhythmic
thrusts against gravity and air . . .

Rather, the silence and almost-stillness of repair:
one woman's fingers probing with the delicate
sanders and brushes, touring the many hand-carved horses,
the one-of-a-kinds of goat, lion, dragon, and deer.
This triple circle of frozen beasts,
more playful than generals or gods in stone,
dwarfs its block-wide park at the city's eye.
Once bright and exotic with colors and shades
the woman can name like family, the carousel
rests worn and chipped by weekend leisure,
by idle hands and feet which gripped and picked and roamed.
The creatures' flanks have suffered heels,
their ears fingers, their saddles knees,
so that now Seattle's homeless gather daily—
however short these several summer weeks—
to watch the giant toy rekindled by lavender,

mauve, umber, brash chromatic yellow,
pine green, pearl, unspellable fuchsia and puce.

If a derelict lifts a hand toward the empty
one-ride midway, might she find her shaky, leathery claw
deserving of compare with the artist's
precisely wired fingers and wrist?
Or is analogy yet another province
traveled only by the fed and settled,
the owners of protein and vitamin B?

The painter talks with every watcher,
her focus deepened by distractions
born of contact. Here is art and politics
wed, beauty and hunger benignly balanced:
her paints and wages are public funds,
yet none of the homeless have wished her gone.

The wealthy come as well, down from their towers
to lounge in the sun that is everyone's dessert,
to shut off their brains for a while,
perhaps to rachet them far enough back to see
the simple, sacred coin in every child's palm—
boss-to-be with nose to the gleaming
windows of trinkets and sweets,
bum-to-be at his leaning, quavering shoulder.

Two Views of Charles Burchfield's Six O'Clock

For Adults: *Where the Painting Is*

You had thought the image was always somewhere else—
people distant or missing, buildings like castles
in air breathed out by exotic, extinct creatures.

But suddenly it is six o'clock, suddenly
Time steps toward you and says, so low, "You know me,
you have walked on my edge between evening and day,

gathered with family as the wall of dark grows hard."
And you see that all this is true, that the tired
moon sagging is a lone sister who shares your bed,

that the bowed heads at the table want food, want rest
you can offer them now that this is your place, your past
become present, this painting a full weight upon your chest.

Look to the blank foreground, whose odd angles speak best:
if your life lacks snow, those shadowed rollings are sea;
if your life is desert, dunes are these low-laid swells;
if your mountain days need mountains, here they are.

Look to the six stark roofs pretending sameness.
None is the same, except as each points its inverted v
skyward, lifting our eyes to that pale gauze
of . . . what? Fog? Smoke? Light? *You* know. You *know*. Out loud.

For Children: *The Painting Comes Home*

So many paintings seem to be somewhere else
in space and time: people are lost in the background
or nowhere in sight, the buildings are like foreign castles.

But here we have home and suppertime,
the air on that edge between day and evening,
the family gathered as the wall of dark grows hard.

These bowed heads at the table simply want food, then rest.
Because you know this place, you can help them
find both. And because you are strong you can lead them

outside to show them so much more: the shadowed yard
whose rolling swells could be waves, dunes, or even mountains;
the six pointed roofs, each slightly different,
lifting toward smoke or fog or cloud;
and that moon, maybe sagging in its lonely wish
to come down and join you, maybe swelling tall
to light the yard and the house for us all.

The Ghost of the Poet

—for Ted Kooser

Top-lit and front-lit, black deep stage behind,
the red and blue pinstripes scant
against the white of your quite-pressed shirt,
you shone like an old-time radio
in a darkened living room,
like the flag in a ballpark's evening glow—
Old Glory hoisted past the massive banks of bulbs
and crisply nailed upon the sky.

You were speaking of the closet skeleton
in any life we could imagine—
"The jaws which bit down hard / on the truth
were stuffed at last / with a velvet glove"—
when I first looked aside and saw your ghost
hanging there at your right hand, my left,
seeming to give off the words you spoke.
He disappeared each time I glanced at you,
came back incandescent when I turned his way.
I listened to his poem of the Goodwill Store,
with its sad and scrounging man we learn is us;
then the specter talked of urine specimens, the small
cupped blessedness of all that's physical—
and so this world, with all its energies,
stepped right back in. I saw your mouthless ghost
in fact was cast by my own staring eyes.
You had ridden light, had moved inside my body.
Your so-clear voice, still yours, was mine.

Emily Dickinson Considers Basketball

In breathing—air is foremost still—
No perfect set of lungs
Makes headway in a vacuum—
Nor sings uncharted songs—

And yet each map is viable
According to its lands—
On fingertips the whorlings
Explain the hearts of hands—

And so this child—in alleyways—
Perfects his picks and shots—
While that one—God's own spotlight takes
To boast his body's cuts.

But both—give me the language—
To speak their passion's moves
As if the fact of motion
Made horses—talk with hooves—

Or angels sing with flutterings
Their tongues need not support—
The round and up and in and out—
Sufficient proof of art—

Stephen Corey's previous poetry collections include *The Last Magician* (Water Mark Press, *1981*), *Synchronized Swimming* (Swallow's Tale Press, *1985*), *All These Lands You Call One Country* (University of Missouri Press, *1992*), *Greatest Hits, 1980-2000* (Pudding House Publications, 2000), and five chapbooks.

His poems, essays, articles, and reviews have appeared in dozens of periodicals and anthologies, among the *The American Poetry Review, Poetry, The Kenyon Review, Yellow Silk, Shenandoah,* and *The Pushcart Prize: Best of the Small Presses.* He has co-edited three books, most recently (with Warren Slesinger) *Spreading the Word: Editors on Poetry* (The Bench Press, *2001*).

In *1976* Corey co-founded *The Devil's Millhopper,* an independent poetry magazine he helped to edit for seven years. Since *1983* he has been on the staff of *The Georgia Review,* for which he is currently associate editor.

Born in Buffalo and reared in Jamestown, New York, Corey was educated at SUNY Binghamton (B.A., M.A.) and the University of Florida (Ph.D.). He lives with his family in Athens, Georgia.